UNDER HIS WINGS

Hymns of Comfort & Hope

ARRANGED FOR SOLO PIANO BY

KATHY SMITH

Moderate

lillenas.com

CONTENTS

O God, Our Help in Ages Past

with

How Firm a Foundation

ISAAC WATTS

WILLIAM CROFT
Arr. by Kathy Smith

1. O God, our Help in ages past,
Our Hope for years to come,
Our Shelter from the stormy blast,
And our eternal Home!

2. Under the shadow of Thy throne
Still may we dwell secure;
Sufficient is Thine arm alone,
And our defense is sure.

3. O God, our Help in ages past,
Our Hope for years to come,
Be Thou our Guide while life shall last,
And our eternal Home.

How firm a foundation, ye saints of the Lord,
Is laid for your faith in His excellent Word!
What more can He say than to you He hath said,
To you who for refuge to Jesus have fled?

*Words John Rippon's Selection of Hymns; Music Traditional American Melody. Arr. © 2011 by Lillenas Publishing Company/SESAC (admin. by Music Services).

26

29

rit.

33

a tempo

38

cresc.

mf

42

8vb

It Is Well with My Soul

HORATIO G. SPAFFORD

PHILIP P. BLISS
Arr. by Kathy Smith

1. When peace like a river attendeth my way,
When sorrows like sea billows roll,
Whatever my lot, Thou hast taught me to say,
"It is well, it is well with my soul."

2. And, Lord, haste the day when the faith shall be sight,
The clouds be rolled back as a scroll,
The trump shall resound and the Lord shall descend.
Even so– it is well with my soul.

Refrain
It is well with my soul.
It is well, it is well with my soul.

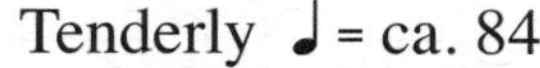

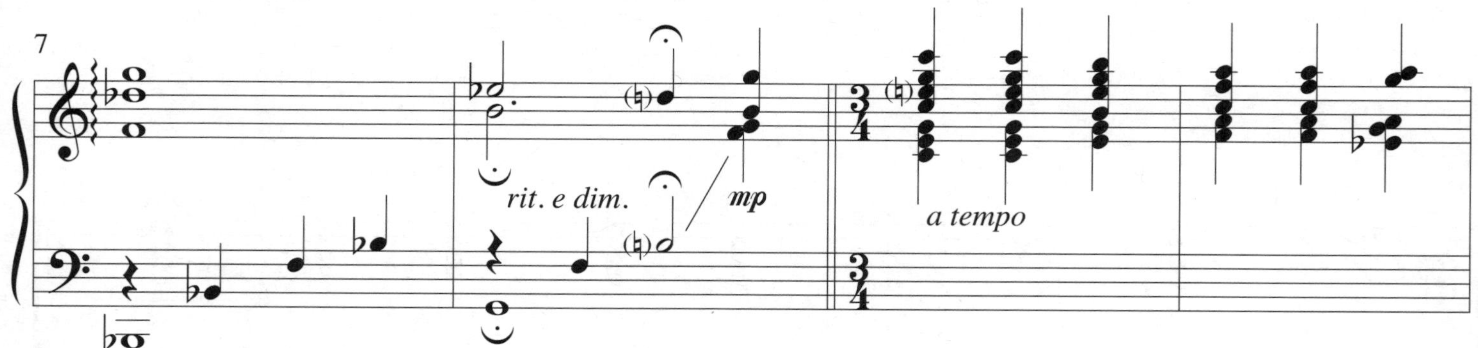

11
14
17
p
mp
p
21
mp
molto rit.
24
ten.
mf a tempo
dim.

27
p
mp
mf
30
ten.
dim.
rit.
molto rit.
ten.
33
mf a tempo
36
cresc.
39
Broadly
f rit.

43
mp
47
mp
p
mp
51
p
mf
54
mp
57

Does Jesus Care?

FRANK E. GRAEFF

J. LINCOLN HALL
Arr. by Kathy Smith

1. Does Jesus care when my heart is pained
Too deeply for mirth and song,
As the burdens press,
And the cares distress,
And the way grows weary and long?

2. Does Jesus care when I've said good-bye
To the dearest on earth to me,
And my sad heart aches
Till it nearly breaks?
Is it aught to Him? Does He see?

Refrain
O yes, He cares; I know He cares!
His heart is touched with my grief.
When the days are weary,
The long nights dreary,
I know my Savior cares.

8
mp
11
rit.
13
cresc.
16
19
rit.
dim.
mp

22
a tempo
mf
rit.
mp a tempo
25
mf
28
Slower ♪ = ca. 72
31
dim.
mp
34
mf
accel.

37
39
rit.
a tempo
42
mp
45

The Lord's My Shepherd

with

Savior, like a Shepherd Lead Us

Scottish Psalter, Psalm 23

JESSE SEYMOUR IRVINE
Arr. by Kathy Smith

1. The Lord's my Shepherd; I'll not want.
He makes me down to lie
In pastures green; He leadeth me
The quiet waters by.

2. Yea, though I walk in death's dark vale,
Yet will I fear no ill;
For Thou art with me, and Thy rod
And staff me comfort still.

3. Goodness and mercy all my life
Shall surely follow me,
And in God's house forevermore
My dwelling place shall be.

*Words *Hymns for the Young*; Music by WILLIAM B. BRADBURY. Arr.

23
28
mf
3
31
34
mp
rit.
37
a tempo

40
cresc.
f
43
47
51
55
mp
rit.
8vb
8vb

Amazing Grace

JOHN NEWTON

Virginia Harmony, 1831
Arr. by Kathy Smith

1. Amazing grace! how sweet the sound
That saved a wretch like me!
I once was lost, but now am found;
Was blind, but now I see.

2. Through many dangers, toils, and snares
I have already come.
'Tis grace hath brought me safe thus far,
And grace will lead me home.

3. When we've been there ten thousand years,
Bright, shining as the sun,
We've no less days to sing God's praise
Than when we'd first begun.

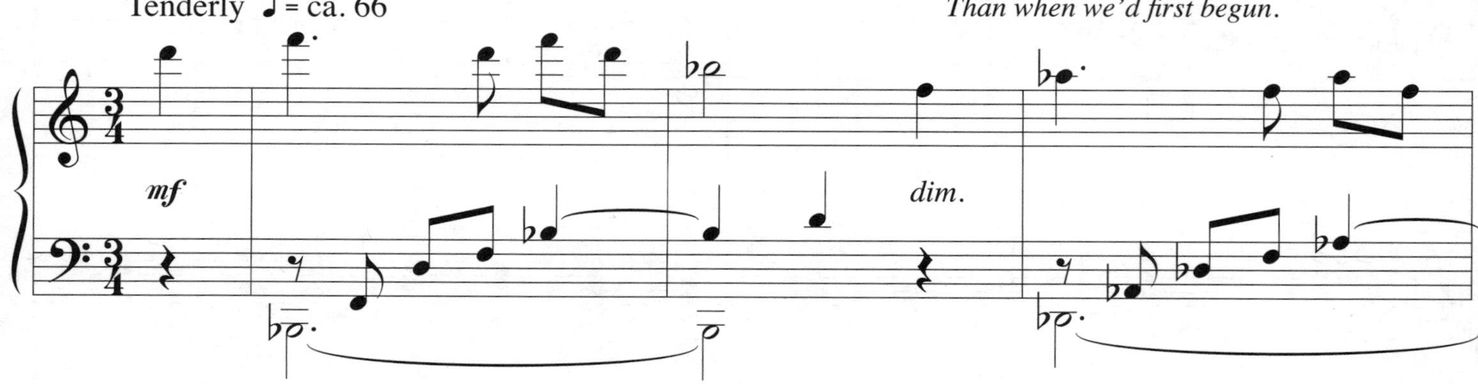

12
3
17
3
21
3
rit.
25
3
p
mp
a tempo
29
3

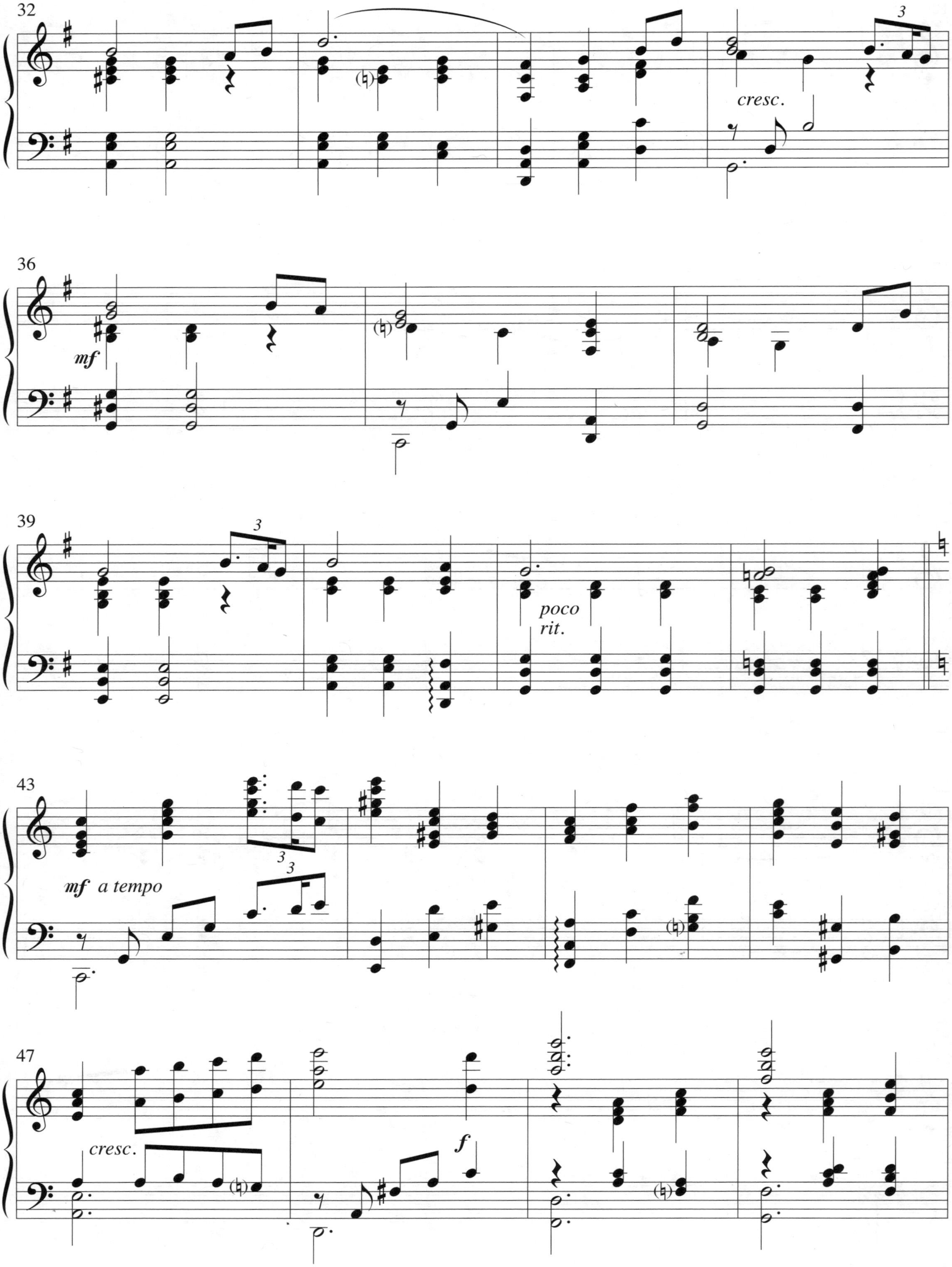
32
3
cresc.
36
mf
39
3
poco
rit.
43
3
3
mf a tempo
47
cresc.
f

51
54
Slowly
3
3
57
8va
mf
dim.
61
mp
64
p
rit.

For All the Saints

WILLIAM W. HOW

RALPH VAUGHAN WILLIAMS
Arr. by Kathy Smith

1. For all the saints who from their labors rest,
Who Thee by faith before the world confessed,
Thy name, O Jesus, be forever blest.
Alleluia! Alleluia!

2. But lo! there breaks a yet more glorious day:
The saints triumphant rise in bright array;
The King of Glory passes on His way.
Alleluia! Alleluia!

3. From earth's wide bounds, from ocean's farthest coast,
Through gates of pearl streams in the countless host,
Singing to Father, Son, and Holy Ghost:
Alleluia! Alleluia!

11
14
17
20
f
23
mf

27
30
33
36
39
f
mf
Broader
f

42
45
48
52
56
mf
rit.

Near to the Heart of God

CLELAND B. MCAFEE

CLELAND B. MCAFEE
Arr. by Kathy Smith

1. There is a place of quiet rest,
Near to the heart of God;
A place where sin cannot molest,
Near to the heart of God.

2. There is a place of comfort sweet,
Near to the heart of God;
A place where we our Savior meet,
Near to the heart of God.

Refrain
O Jesus, blest Redeemer,
Sent from the heart of God,
Hold us, who wait before Thee,
Near to the heart of God.

Pensively, freely ♩ = ca. 63

mp

4

rit. mf

a tempo

7

10
13
16
18
mp
rit.
20
cresc.
mf a tempo

22

24

26

28

31

34
rit.
p
37
39
42
mp
44
rit.

Under His Wings

WILLIAM O. CUSHING

IRA D. SANKEY
Arr. by Kathy Smith

1. Under His wings I am safely abiding.
Though the night deepens and tempests are wild,
Still I can trust Him; I know He will keep me.
He has redeemed me, and I am His child.

2. Under His wings, what a refuge in sorrow!
How the heart yearningly turns to His rest!
Often when earth has no balm for my healing,
There I find comfort, and there I am blest.

Refrain
Under His wings, under His wings,
Who from His love can sever?
Under His wings my soul shall abide,
Safely abide forever.

7
9
mf
11
13
cresc.
mf
15
dim.
mp

17
pp
mel.
mp
19
ten.
ten.
mp
ten.
ten.
21
mel.
cresc.
mf
dim.
mp
23
25
mf

28
cresc.
dim.
31
mp
p
34
mp
pp
mel.
mp
36
rit.
a tempo
mf
38
ten.
dim.
ten.
mp rit.
p

What a Friend We Have in Jesus

with

In the Garden

JOSEPH M. SCRIVEN

CHARLES C. CONVERSE
Arr. by Kathy Smith

What a Friend we have in Jesus,
All our sins and griefs to bear!
What a privilege to carry
Everything to God in prayer!
O what peace we often forfeit,
O what needless pain we bear,
All because we do not carry
Everything to God in prayer!

Have we trials and temptations?
Is there trouble anywhere?
We should never be discouraged;
Take it to the Lord in prayer.
Can we find a friend so faithful
Who will all our sorrows share?
Jesus knows our every weakness;
Take it to the Lord in prayer.

*Words and Music by C. AUSTIN MILES.